Original title:
Beyond the Island Breeze

Copyright © 2025 Creative Arts Management OÜ
All rights reserved.

Author: Ronan Whitfield
ISBN HARDBACK: 978-1-80581-684-3
ISBN PAPERBACK: 978-1-80581-211-1
ISBN EBOOK: 978-1-80581-684-3

Serendipity in the Swells

A crab in a hat, what a sight,
He jives on the sand, quite the delight.
With waves as his dance floor, he twirls and spins,
Chuckling at seagulls, their laughter he wins.

Caught in a wave, a flip-flop flies,
A swim lesson gone wrong, oh how time flies!
With sunburned noses, we lay back to bake,
The ocean's a giggle, oh, what a mistake!

The Horizon Calls to Wanderers

A lighthouse whispers jokes to the boats,
While dolphins dive, wearing little coats.
The salty breeze tickles our noses so sweet,
As we chase after crabs on our sunburned feet.

The sunset paints faces with orange and pink,
While we ponder life over cool drinks, we think.
An octopus waves, sporting a fine hat,
Its fancy attire makes us all laugh at that!

Lullabies of the Lapping Waves

The waves sing softly, a rhythm divine,
As turtles glide slowly, they sip on fine wine.
"Why hurry?" they say, as they drift with a grin,
In their slow-motion dance, who needs to win?

The seaweed wiggles, it tickles our toes,
While minnows all gather for gossip and prose.
The starfish strike poses, so bold and so brave,
Creating a splash as they tumble and wave!

Sunlit Journeys Across the Cove

We paddle our craft, with a goose as our guide,
While watching our snacks take a slippery slide.
The fish start to giggle, they know we'll lose track,
As seagulls dive down for the forgotten snack.

The sun's shining bright, we start to sunbathe,
While floating on rafts, we joke and we rave.
With belly laughs rolling, what stories unfold,
In this paradise, there's no need to be bold!

A Canvas of Coral and Cloud

In colors bright, the fish do dance,
A clown tried swimming, but lost his pants!
The seaweed sways, with giggles loud,
Even crabs have humor, oh so proud.

Seagulls swoop in, mischief at play,
Snatching snacks, then flying away.
A crab yells out, 'Hey, that's my fry!'
But the gull just grins, and off he'll fly!

Whispers of the Windswept Coast

The wind tells tales of a silly seal,
Who wore a hat and tried to heal.
He slipped on sand, right onto his back,
A flip-flop landing—now that's off track!

The laughter echoes along the bay,
As fish gossip about the clumsy play.
A dolphin chuckles, 'Look at him flop!'
But soon they all join—let's have a bop!

The Lure of Untamed Shores

Barefoot we scamper along the strand,
Finding treasures all made of sand.
A crab rolls past with a tiny crown,
Declares himself king, no need to frown!

The waves crash, and we leap with glee,
A misfit pirate next to a tree.
He strikes a pose, with a rubber sword,
Pretends to conquer, and we applaud!

Shadows of Forgotten Sunsets

The twilight brings a silly sight,
A penguin waddles, oh what a fright!
Trip over rocks with a goofy smile,
Does a little dance—let's stay a while!

As shadows stretch, whispers take flight,
A parrot squawks, 'This party's tight!'
With laughter shared, we all agree,
Even the sunset has humor, you see!

Secrets Held in Surging Foam

Waves whisper tales with a giggle,
Seagulls swoop down, trying to wiggle.
I lost my hat in a playful splash,
And the fish all laughed, what a bash!

Sandcastles crumbled with a loud thud,
While crabs in tuxedos danced in mud.
The tide brought in a sponge on a spree,
Said, "Life's a party, come join me!"

The Promise of Another Shore

A beach ball rolled like a runaway pup,
Chasing the breeze as I filled my cup.
A flip-flop flew, with a comical twist,
The sun just winked at the hilarity missed.

Sandy toes and sunscreen smiles,
As we slide down dunes, it's all worth the miles.
The jellyfish jiggled, a gooey delight,
And in this chaos, everything feels right.

Footprints in Ephemeral Sand

We leave marks that fade with each tide's kiss,
Running from seagulls, it's pure summer bliss.
I tripped on a starfish, oh what a sight!
And laughed as it waved, all covered in light.

Each step we take, a giggly ballet,
Turns into splashes; let's swim, hip-hip-hooray!
With laughter echoing, we dance on the shore,
Chasing the tides — who could ask for more?

Rhythms of Sea and Sky

The ocean croons with a playful note,
While clouds join in, wearing their best coat.
Fish flip-flop like they're stars of a show,
As I try to dance, but just end up in woe.

Surfboards wobble on waves that sway,
As dolphins poke fun, on this fine day.
Every splash a duet, a whimsical tune,
We're all just merry fools under the moon!

Reflections of Celestial Quitude

Beneath the starry sky so bright,
A crab does dance, what a funny sight!
He twirls and spins, a sandy twister,
Chasing his dreams, oh what a mister!

The moon is laughing, gleeful and round,
While fish in the tide play hide and bound,
A jellyfish floats, a balloon on a spree,
Wobbling along like a friend at tea!

The Journey of the Wandering Gull

A gull takes flight with a sandwich in beak,
He squawks at the beach, oh such a cheek!
He dives for a fry, then snags a chip,
While beachgoers laugh, and the seagulls trip!

With friends in tow, they chase the sun,
Plucking popcorn, oh what fun!
A flip and a flop, they dive with glee,
These feathered jesters hold the key!

Promises Written in Ocean Currents

The waves write tales on sandy shores,
Of coconut dances and surfboard roars,
A clam whispers secrets to a passing shell,
As kites tumble high, weaving ocean's spell!

Frogs wear sunglasses, croaking in style,
Throwing a beach party, oh what a dial!
With ocean breeze tickling every fin,
The laughter rolls in like a playful din!

The Heartbeat of the Tidal Dunes

In the dunes, the wind has a silly muse,
It tickles the grass, gives it a ruse,
A tumbleweed rolls, with a whirl and a laugh,
While critters come out for a dance and a chaff!

The sands dance joyfully, shifting their tunes,
As crickets serenade beneath the moons,
With a hop and a skip, the dunes give a cheer,
In this playful realm, nothing to fear!

Where the Sky and Water Meet

Where sea and sky collide, oh what a sight,
Fish in tuxedos dance, oh what a delight.
Seagulls gossip up high, with sandy old tales,
While crabs in the tide wear their curious scales.

The sun wears a crown, all golden and bright,
As waves try to tickle the gulls in flight.
"Hey you, fish!" they squawk with a flappy flair,
While dolphins in bow ties perform in mid-air.

Sails Against a Blushing Sky

Sails on the horizon, bright colors and cheer,
Boats competing for top spot, each captain austere.
Wave-riding turtles yell, "We're winning the race!"
While pirates wear swim trunks, proclaiming "This place!"

A breeze brings a fart, oh what a surprise,
Even the fish cover their pint-sized eyes.
The sun blinks in laughter, as waves roll with glee,
Each puff of sea breath smells like jellyfish tea!

Starlit Paths Over the Water

Stars above giggle, they twinkle with glee,
As fish swim in patterns, playing hide and seek.
Moonbeams throw parties on the shimmering tide,
While waves share their secrets, the ocean confides.

A crab tells a joke about a traveling seal,
Whose boat sprung a leak; it's hard to conceal!
The night-time whispers giggles through ships,
As sailors shoot marshmallows and take silly sips.

The Language of Ocean Breezes

Breezes chatter softly, with whispers of fun,
"Hey there, you blushing waves, can't we all run?"
The sea foam chuckles, tickling the shore,
While wind plays the kazoo, wanting nothing more.

Fish throw a beach ball, a splashy surprise,
While shells roll their eyes at the contorting skies.
Seagulls laugh loudly, while pelicans dive,
In this wacky water world, the joy is alive!

Horizons That Call to the Heart

A seagull steals my sandwich,
The tides giggle in delight,
I chase it down the shoreline,
While sunscreen ruins my sight.

My friends laugh as I stumble,
Tripping over seashells galore,
I swear they're out to get me,
This beach, a prankster's floor.

A crab waves like a madman,
I answer with a silly dance,
The waves clap like a drummer,
We share a quirky trance.

And as the sun sets below,
I plop down with an ice cream cone,
The horizon smiles wide and bright,
In this chaos, I feel at home.

Solitude in the Misty Expanse

In a quiet corner, I ponder,
Misty waves blot the view,
I thought I'd find my zen here,
But I'm wrestling with a shoe.

Each wave whispers a riddle,
My towel flaps like a flag,
Seagulls steal my thoughts away,
And my umbrella turns to snag.

I tried to catch a clumsy breeze,
But it giggled, tugged, and spun,
Now I'm tangled in a hammock,
Sipping on that last hot bun.

Silence wraps around me tight,
Yet I trip on my own thoughts,
Laughter hides within each wave,
In solitude, chaos is taught.

When the Wind Speaks in Secrets

The wind whispers sweet nonsense,
Tickling my shores with glee,
I ask it, "What do you say?"
It replies, "Just let it be!"

A kite flies off with my hat,
A squirrel joins the fun parade,
Together we dance in the sunlight,
To the rhythm of shade and jade.

I yell at the waves, "Come closer!"
But they just splash and retreat,
Are they playing hard to get?
This game's whimsical and sweet.

As twilight paints the horizon,
I join the battle for lost socks,
Whispers and giggles entwined,
With wind-blown melodies, it rocks.

Memories of a Forgotten Cove

In a cove where laughter echoes,
I found a treasure chest of fun,
Just old socks and half a sandwich,
But hey, I'm easily won!

A crab tries to steal my flip-flop,
I chase it, both running wild,
This beach, a portrait of madness,
Where every moment feels like a child.

A sea turtle gives me a wink,
As I fumble with my board,
We share a laugh at the surf's edge,
In harmony, we're both restored.

But when the tide carries away,
My bucket dreams and sandy lore,
I wave goodbye with a chuckle,
And promise to return for more.

Canvas of Shifting Shadows

In a world where shadows dance,
Laughter swirls in every glance.
A parrot sings a witty tune,
While crabs in coats strut at noon.

With sun hats perched on tiny heads,
They giggle over tourist spreads.
Oh, what a sight, these creatures bold,
Fashion tips worth more than gold!

The surfboards wear a silly grin,
As waves tease at their silly fins.
A jellyfish in spectacles bright,
Claims he's the star of the beach tonight!

So grab your shades and join the fray,
As shadows shift in playful sway.
With every twist, there's joy anew,
A canvas painted just for you!

The Haunting Call of Distant Shores

A ghostly whale sings from afar,
His jolly tunes carry like a car.
With flip-flops flying, splashes abound,
It's a seaside bash, all around!

The sandcastles rise up like dreams,
Each with moat and marshmallow beams.
But watch out! A seagull takes a bite,
Of the royal jelly on the knight!

Mermaids laugh from rocky ledges,
As octopuses play with hedges.
They tip their hats and do a jig,
Inviting all for a playful gig!

So heed the call from distant lands,
Join in the fun with sandy hands.
For every wave that whispers near,
Is laced with giggles and hearty cheer!

Solitude in Swaying Palms

A coconut winks from its perch so high,
Challenging folks to reach for the sky.
The palms sway low, then reach for the sun,
While squirrels debate who's stealing the fun.

One crab does yoga, striking a pose,
While the other one snoozes, blissfully dozed.
It's a solo act in a crowd so grand,
With nature's humor at every hand.

The breeze whispers secrets of the wise,
As seagulls exchange the latest lies.
They laugh at the tides that twist and twirl,
Creating a surfboard of laughs to unfurl!

In shadows of palms, let your worries go,
For laughter and light are the sweetest flow.
So find your joy in the sunny sway,
And dance with the breeze all through the day!

Melodies Carried by the Sea

Driftwood strums a salty tune,
As crabs tap dance under the moon.
A starfish conductor leads the way,
Orchestrating fun at the end of the day.

Seashells gossip, sharing old tales,
Of lazy fish and wind-blown sails.
Every wave sings a merry rhyme,
As laughter echoes through the brine.

The dolphins leap with cheeky cheer,
Flipping over waves without a fear.
They challenge whales to a silly race,
In the ocean's grand and goofy space!

So come and join the coastal spree,
Where melodies drift like honeyed tea.
With every splash and every glee,
Life's a comedy on the open sea!

Embracing the Nautical Night

The stars above are quite the sight,
A sailor's hat that fits just right.
With pranks and gags, we sail the tide,
A fish named Bob, our crew's great pride.

The moonlight shadows sparkle bright,
As we giggle and chase the light.
A seagull squawks with quite a flair,
Wearing a scarf, it claims the air.

We spin the wheel, we laugh and cheer,
While juggling crabs and downing beer.
The compass points in circles round,
Our path leads only to the ground!

So here we are, a motley crew,
In laughter's grip, this night's our due.
With waves that dance, we feel so free,
A floating circus on the sea!

Crushed Seashells and Forgotten Dreams

On sandy shores, where dreams run wild,
We gather shells, just like a child.
With crushed shells, our pockets full,
We prize strange treasures, what a haul!

Forgotten dreams like driftwood waste,
We build a castle, what a taste!
A moat of jellyfish nearby,
They guard our feast with a squishy cry.

The crabs hold court, they clap and cheer,
As we toast to our best idea.
A rock star clam, on stage tonight,
Though it's pitchy, we call it bright!

With laughter winks and silly schemes,
We dance beneath the moon's soft beams.
From crushed shells, new dreams arise,
A symphony beneath the skies!

Secrets Buried Under Waves

Beneath the waves, secrets do sleep,
Where fishy tales and mermaids leap.
We dive down deep for hidden loot,
But find a boot and a garden gnome too!

With snorkels on, we scour the deep,
For treasures lost, our hearts to keep.
Neptune laughs, his beard a mess,
As we flounder 'round—a tight dress!

The octopus seems quite bemused,
As we scramble about, slightly confused.
Its eight legs dance, a jolly display,
While we giggle and float away.

So if you're down where secrets hide,
Keep giggling softly, with fins as your guide.
In waves like whispers, joy prevails,
In oceans deep, where mirth never fails!

The Drift of the Ocean's Heart

Sailing forth on a whimsy breeze,
With wacky hats that dance with ease.
The ocean's heart starts to sway,
Catch the drift, it leads our way!

A dolphin laughs, it jumps and plays,
With bubble rings in silly ways.
We join in, flapping arms so wide,
In a dance-off with the tide.

The seaweed waltzes, swaying slow,
While starfish clap in a gentle row.
With each wave, a chuckle shared,
A party boat with no one prepared!

So let the ocean guide our feet,
In zany steps, our joy's complete.
As laughter echoes far and near,
The heart of the sea brings endless cheer!

A Seafarer's Heartbeat

In a boat with a squeak, I sail with glee,
The fish they all laugh, just like me.
Waves tickle my toes, they dance with cheer,
Oh, give me a laugh, and I'll steer clear.

A seagull swoops down, hungry for fries,
I toss him a roll, much to my surprise.
He squawks like a sailor, a hoot and a jest,
Swapping my lunch, he says it's the best.

With a parrot on deck, we sing a loud tune,
Trying to catch crabs, what a buffoon!
They pinch at my ankles, I holler and shout,
A seafarer's life has its quirks, no doubt.

As the stars take the stage in the sky's grand show,
I ponder my fortune, this wild ebb and flow.
For laughter's the treasure that sails with me,
In this quirky life, oh, I'm truly free!

Drifted Memories Along the Coast

On the shore, I once tripped, lost my flip-flop,
Found a clamshell hat, that's quite the hop!
Seagulls squabble over my forgotten snack,
Whipping up chaos, like a tidal attack.

Tanned sunburned skin, I sport like a crab,
All pink and splotchy, don't I look fab?
Waves wash my worries, a slap to the face,
But nothing quite beats this sandy embrace.

A sandcastled kingdom, I build with pride,
But a rogue wave laughs, and it slips and slides.
The tide brings my troubles but washes 'em out,
In this playful world, I can laugh and shout.

As sunset's glow bathes the evening sky,
I dance with the waves, as they ripple by.
Memories drift like shells upon the sand,
With joy in my heart, I'm in this grand land!

Echoes of Time in the Tides

The tide pulls my humor like an old joke,
A crab with a cane gives a wise little poke.
Shells whisper secrets, of days long ago,
Echoes of laughter, in waves' gentle flow.

A fish with a grin swims past with a quirk,
He winks as he passes, he's quite the jerk.
Dolphins play tag, splashing all around,
In a silly circus, I'm lost, truly found.

Old lighthouse chuckles, beacon of light,
As the waves roll in, creating pure delight.
With seagulls for friends, and a splash for a smile,
I'm wrapped in the joy, in this watery isle.

Each moment a giggle, each wave a new chance,
In the heart of the ocean, I twirl and prance.
Echoes of laughter, resounding in sand,
In this funny tidal dance, I forever stand!

A Journey Through Marine Mysteries

Setting sail at dawn, with coffee in hand,
I spy a strange fish, oh, it's far from bland.
With feathers on fins and a joke to recite,
Marine mysteries await, what a sight!

The octopus grins, wearing socks of bright hues,
He plays peek-a-boo, while I sip my brew.
From the deep blue abyss, the laughter erupts,
In this zany realm, even sharks make us chump.

A treasure map drawn with crayon and flair,
Leads to buried snacks, hidden with care.
Oh, the sea's full of riddles and giggles galore,
Every wave brings a whimsy, an opening door.

As the tide whispers tales of the fun we unfurl,
I know in my heart, I'll savor each swirl.
Through slippery antics, this journey I cherish,
With laughter my compass, I'll never perish!

The Art of Letting Go on Waves

Surfboards dance, they trip and fall,
Tanned bods tumble, a watery brawl.
A seagull swoops to steal my fries,
I laugh, surrendering to ocean sighs.

Catch the wave or catch a cold,
The sun's too bright, the tales too bold.
Fins and flippers in chaos sway,
Each splash a giggle in sun's array.

A Refuge from the World's Clamor

Crabs in sunglasses, chillin' like pros,
While surfers argue which way the tide goes.
Flip-flops squeak on the sandy highway,
As beach towels dance, they join the play.

The cooler's stocked with snacks galore,
"Did you bring the salsa?" "No, just more!"
Laughter spills like the waves that crash,
While sunscreen's lost in a wild splash.

The Hidden Stories of the Surf

Every wave whispers, "Did you see?"
A dolphin flips, it's comedy!
Sandcastles rise with a royal flair,
Till a wave comes in, "Ha! Not a care!"

The salty breeze tells tales of old,
Of sunburnt lessons and treasures bold.
Shells with secrets lie underfoot,
As gulls squawk cheap jokes, without a boot.

Timeless Threads of the Ocean's Weave

Fishing nets tangle in laughter's choke,
With every cast, a humorous joke.
Starfish gossip of lands far away,
While sea turtles sip drinks, enjoying the day.

The waves roll in with giggles anew,
Dragging shoreline dreams, some very askew.
Life's a beach ball, round and spry,
In the arms of the sea, we laugh, oh my!

The Dance of Sun-kissed Waves

The waves are bouncing, what a sight,
They dance and twirl, oh, what delight!
A seagull joins, with a silly glide,
While crabs do the cha-cha, filled with pride.

Flip-flops fly as kids all run,
Splashing water, such silly fun!
A beach ball soars, then lands askew,
The lifeguard laughs, 'Is that a shoe?'

With sand castles crumbling in the breeze,
A tiny kingdom made with ease.
But watch out now, don't let it drown,
A wave brings down the hottest crown!

So here we are, in sunlit cheer,
With laughter loud, a joyful sphere.
As sun sets low, we'll reminisce,
About goofy waves and ocean bliss.

Reflections on a Serene Shore

The tide rolls in, it takes a peek,
What glimmers there? A silver sheik!
A bottle floats, like treasure near,
Inside, a note that reads, 'Have beer!'

A sandy dog with shades so bright,
Is lounging hard, what pure delight!
He snickers at the surfers' falls,
As they tumble and make awkward calls.

The sun-kissed path, a trail of fun,
I trip and tumble, now there's a pun!
The seagulls cackle, their beaks so sly,
"Next time, try to aim, oh my!"

As beachgoers chat and munch on treats,
The sand sticks here, there, and in pleats.
But oh! It's worth it, for laughs and cheer,
We'll do it again, same time next year!

A Symphony of Seashells

A crab with flair conducts the band,
In a shell concert, off the sand!
Clams do a jig, and oysters sing,
While starfish twirl, oh what a thing!

A conch blows loud, it's quite a sound,
The gulls join in, they're all around.
"Encore! Encore!" we all will shout,
As fish join in without a doubt.

The tide pools bubble with giggles galore,
As seaweed sways, a leafy chore.
A clam snaps shut, with a clever wink,
"I'm not your prop, so don't you think!"

The concert ends with a soft splash,
As creatures bow, we give a crash!
In shells we trust, for laughs and glee,
This symphony of joy, eternally.

Driftwood Shadows in the Sand

Driftwood lies like art on the shore,
A twisted stick, but wait—there's more!
A crab has claimed it, made it his throne,
He waves at me, "I'm not alone!"

The shadows dance as the sun dips low,
And whispers rise from the sea's soft flow.
"Come join the party!" says a book of sand,
"Just watch out for the rogue sprinkler hand!"

The kids are weaving with sticks and strings,
Creating instruments that wobble and sing.
But what's that sound? A splashing spree!
The driftwood's laughing along with glee.

As night descends with a twinkling flair,
We gather close, without a care.
With stories spun from shadowy dawn,
We celebrate, till the night is gone.

Tales Weaved in Ocean Winds

In the surf, we spin our yarns,
Of fish that dance like silly clowns,
The seagulls squawk, they eavesdrop,
While sandcastles wear funny crowns.

Crabs in hats parade with pride,
Each wave a jest, a playful ride,
The dolphins giggle, splash around,
In our laughter, joy is found.

We chase the tide, it runs away,
With every quip, our spirits sway,
Shells whisper jokes beneath the sun,
While ocean's chuckles have just begun.

So raise a toast with coconut drinks,
To stories we give silly shrinks,
In salty air, we find our muse,
While the sea laughs at our goofy views.

The Solace of Salted Whispers

Salted breezes carry tales,
Of mermaids who ride tiny snails,
Their laughter echoes 'round the shore,
As ocean waves beg for encore.

Octopus on stilts struts so grand,
Waves tickle toes stuck in the sand,
Jellyfish join in with bright lights,
They dance till the starry nights.

We toss our worries to the tide,
With seaweed wiggles as our guide,
A chorus of crabs join our song,
In this paradise, we all belong.

So grab your board and join the fun,
The salty joy has just begun,
With smiles as bright as ocean's blue,
We find solace in laughter too.

Heartbeats Beneath Mystic Waters

Beneath the waves, the jelly waltz,
Where fish share secrets, that's no false,
They tickle pink our every thought,
With bubbles making laughter caught.

Starfish flip like smiles in tide,
While clams narrate, we sit inside,
The ocean's floor is quite the stage,
Where silly sea creatures engage.

We sneak a peek at dolphins' tease,
As they're throwing finny parties with ease,
Their splashes spray our giggles high,
Beneath the surface, we float and sigh.

With every heartbeat, joy takes flight,
In this watery world of pure delight,
So join the fun, make waves of glee,
In the heartbeat of the sea, we're free.

Where Dreams Interlace with Seafoam

In frothy dreams, we chase the squish,
As seafoam dips and takes a swish,
Shells gossip sweet, with tales galore,
Of pirates who lost their socks on shore.

The playful tide winks with a tease,
We catch quick laughs with every breeze,
Starfish tap dance on the wet sand,
In the whimsy, we take our stand.

Seagulls swoop with goofy shrieks,
Joining our fun as humor peaks,
The surf brings jokes on gentle waves,
Where every laugh is what one craves.

So gather 'round, let stories flow,
In seafoam's arms, our spirits glow,
Where dreams and laughter weave and play,
In the ocean's heart, we find our way.

Whispers of the Ocean Mist

Seagulls squawk, on diets of fries,
Chasing a sandwich, oh, what a prize!
The waves laugh softly, a ticklish sound,
As crabs strut sideways, looking profound.

A fish in sunglasses, just took a dive,
It flexes its fins, feeling so alive.
The tide takes its time, but oh, what a show,
With shells making music, a conch-tastic flow.

A wave rolled in, gave the beach a hug,
Then slipped on a seaweed, oh what a shrug!
The sand castles grin, their turrets so high,
As kids stomp through them, with a gleeful cry.

In the distance, a dolphin does prance,
Trying to dance in a fishy romance.
And the sun winks down, a mischievous sprite,
As laughter and splashes fade into night.

Secrets of the Distant Shore

The crabs hold council, plotting a feast,
While turtles play tag, not caring in the least.
A clam with a shell, the size of a moon,
Swears it once dated a dolphin named June.

Seashells gossip, their stories so wild,
About lost flip-flops and a sunbaked child.
The breeze carries laughter, thick like a stew,
As sandcastles topple, oh, what a view!

A seagull steals fries, oh what a bold move,
While tourists look on, not sure how to groove.
And the waves tease the shore, with whispers so spry,
As the tide trips over, like waves in July.

A treasure chest hidden, but only a sock,
The pirates have gold, but this feels like a knock!
And the sun sets with oranges, pinks, and deep blues,
As laughter and fun bring sweet evening hues.

Echoes of the Wandering Tides

A crab with a crown, struts like a king,
While the fish throw a party, they dance, they sing!
The dolphins flip-flop, all gleaming and bright,
Under bubbles that shimmer, reflecting the light.

A snail on a surfboard, oh, what a sight!
Trying to catch the waves with all its might.
The jellyfish jive, in a squishy ballet,
As the ocean keeps laughing, day after day.

The beaches hold secrets, from coffers of sand,
A sock, an old shoe — oh, what a grand brand!
Together they giggle as the tides roll and roll,
Ballet dancing under the moon's shining scroll.

The seagulls debate, 'Do we fly or we feast?'
While children build castles, and laugh like a beast!
And when twilight whispers, all sweet and low,
We dance with the tides, oh what a show!

Serenade of the Sunlit Horizon

The sun wakes up, with a fuzzy hairdo,
As crabs in bowties play timeless taboo.
A dog on the shore rolls in sea's embrace,
While flip-flops swim freely, oh what a chase!

The seagulls plot mischief, their eyes all aglow,
As they dive for that sandwich, a perfect tableau.
Buckets of laughter, and sand flying high,
The beach is a circus, oh me, oh my!

The tide pulls its pranks, leaving footprints like art,
They're masterpieces faded, but fill up the heart.
And just as we wave, to the sun at its peak,
The day laughs back, with a sunburned cheek.

As the breeze tells secrets, of grand escapades,
And the saltwater tickles, the softest parades.
In the twilight's embrace, we spin and we run,
Finding joy in the whispers, of a day just begun.

Remnants of Twilight's Caress

Sunset giggles, clouds in disguise,
A seagull's waltz, beneath berry pies.
Crabs don sunglasses, they strut with flair,
While starfish snap photos, unaware of despair.

Coconut shells play a game of their own,
Dancing mermaids claim the sea foam throne.
A fish wearing glasses swims sideways with glee,
While the tide whispers secrets to the jellyfish spree.

Laughter lingers where the ocean waves tease,
As octopuses juggle, doing just as they please.
The moon cracks jokes, casting shadows so wide,
While the beach bum sunbaths, waves rolling his ride.

In twilight's embrace, all worries are lost,
For silliness blooms at the strangest of costs.
With laughter like bubbles, rising and free,
Each chuckle a splash, in this oceanic spree.

Melancholy in the Coral Reefs

A clownfish sighs, lips pouting so wide,
He's lost in his thoughts, it's a turbulent tide.
A turtle named Steve wears a hat on his head,
While corals gossip, adding to his dread.

Sardines slip by, in a hurried retreat,
As sea cucumbers giggle, not feeling the heat.
They ponder their lives, in this swirling ballet,
With jellyfish holding their own cabaret.

The whale hums soft tunes, feeling forlorn,
While a lobster frets, his new shell is worn.
A crab writes his memoirs, in the sand in a sprawl,
As sea urchins nod along, not caring at all.

Though sadness arrives with the soft ocean breeze,
Humor will sprout where the water's at ease.
For beneath the waves, with a wink and a twist,
Joy dances freely, even when mist is kissed.

Trails of Stars on the Water's Surface

Glittering ripples, a canvas of light,
A fish blinks twice, joking into the night.
Stars do the cha-cha on the waves' gentle crest,
While dolphins spin tales that put dreams to the test.

The moon, in a top hat, winks with delight,
As otters perform in the cool silver light.
With splashes and giggles, the night fills with cheer,
Even crabs in the shadows can't manage a sneer.

A boat drifts by, carrying laughter and cries,
With a parrot named Jerry, who mimics the skies.
He quips about fish, and the weight of their swag,
While pirates tell tales of the treasure they drag.

In a swirl of bright colors, joy claims its due,
While the tides hum a tune, under skies deep and blue.
With trails of soft laughter, the sea will restore,
The whimsy of waters, forever to explore.

The Aroma of Distant Adventures

Tropical breezes carry scents of the past,
With pineapples dreaming of leaves, oh so vast.
A banana boat sails, its pals all aglee,
While mangoes discuss life, as sweet as can be.

The sun whispers secrets to busy coconuts,
As crabs wear top hats, holding silly ruts.
A parrot squawks loudly, 'Did you see that big wave?'
With laughter like thunder, it's our balls they save.

Palm trees sway wildly, sharing inside jokes,
As fish in tuxedos dance like clumsy folks.
A piña colada does the shimmy and shake,
While the truth of the matter, no one dares take.

In every breeze swirling, new tales will be spun,
With aromas of laughter, the day's just begun.
So raise up your coconuts, cheer under the sky,
For far-away travels, with each pulse of the tide!

Journeys to the Edge of Water

We sailed on a float, made of old cans,
With dreams in our pockets and sunburned plans.
The map said go left, but we turned to the right,
Chasing a seagull that looked like a knight.

The waves laughed at us, tossed us around,
As fish performed pirouettes, so profound.
We caught a big splash, and our hats flew away,
Now jellyfish wear them, quite the cabaret!

The compass was faulty, or maybe it lied,
We feasted on sandwiches as gulls circled wide.
I tried to catch one, but it flew with a wink,
While I ended up drenched, all I could do was blink.

We laughed at our journey to places unknown,
With memories formed in the salty sea foam.
What taught us to navigate, no one could steer,
Just a taco truck's bell ringing louder than fear!

Tales Carried by the Tide

On shores where the crabs threw a dance quite bizarre,
I tried to be stealthy, but I tripped on a star.
The tide rolled in laughing, a wave's cheeky prank,
Made sandcastles tumble, oh dear, what a sank!

We gathered our shells, each one with a tale,
One told of a fish who rode on a whale.
Another was grumpy, it clacked and it scolded,
Said beachgoers' footprints had him much too folded.

The seaweed did tango, in rhythms so funny,
While we all just giggled, their dance wasn't phony.
A surfer lost balance, his board took a dive,
He came up with seaweed, "A new way to thrive!"

And as the sun set, casting shadows so wide,
We shared all our stories, with laughter as our guide.
These tales carried by water, in waves they abound,
A beach full of chuckles, forever profound!

Tranquility in Temporary Havens

We set up our tent, on a rock but no spot,
A sandwich named Larry, our lunch on a plot.
The wind played a trick, blew our snacks to the bay,
Now fish are quite full, in a very fine way!

With sand in our shoes and hats on askew,
We fished for our fortune, the flops yes, the crew!
A turtle named Gary paddled by with great flair,
Said, "Join my slow race," and we all got a scare!

A hammock we strung, between two old trees,
While squirrels held a meeting, discussing the bees.
Their chatter was lively, a comedy show,
With nut jokes and puns they tossed to and fro.

At dusk, we just giggled, in laughter we stayed,
While crickets now played our serenade.
The night wrapped us up, in its hug soft and tight,
In our temporary haven, we danced through the night!

The Rhythm of Rolling Fathoms

A boat like spaghetti rode waves quite beguiled,
With a captain who squeaked when the sea winds reviled.
We spun in circles, our compass was rare,
The whales joined our band, with a flip and a flair.

With laughter and splashes, the sea hit our dreams,
As dolphins threw parties, with bubbles and beams.
I tried to sing bass, but it came out as squeaks,
While octopuses giggled, as they helped with our beats.

On a treasure map, X marked, perhaps twice,
The pirate turned out to be not so precise.
We found that the 'gold' was a chest full of snacks,
Chocolate and gummies rolled tight in neat packs.

As twilight framed our ocean so blue,
We danced with the fish, and the moon joined the crew.
The rhythm of waves, with our hearts all aligned,
In this wobbly life of humor, we'll always find!

The Enchantment of Shimmering Shores

A crab in a tuxedo scuttles right past,
Cracking jokes, he's quite the comical cast.
Seagulls are laughing, a raucous delight,
Their squawking like laughter, a humorous sight.

The waves they are dancing, so carefree and bold,
Splashing at sunbathers, oh, they'll never be sold.
A beach ball goes flying, it lands with a thud,
While sunscreened folks giggle, all smothered in mud.

The sandcastle towers rise high in the air,
Until a rogue seagull swoops down with a flair.
"Oh no!" shouts the builder, "it's my finest work!"
But the bird only chuckles, a mischievous jerk.

As the sun sets low, painting skies in bright hues,
Fishermen's tales spin like glittering shoes.
With laughter resounding, the night comes alive,
On these shores of enchantment, where joy can thrive.

Beneath the Silvered Moonlight

The moon's a big cookie, all shiny and bright,
While fish in tuxedos swim left then to right.
A dolphin with glitter, he jumps with a grin,
Says, "Join in my party, let's all dive in!"

Starfish play piano, they're quite the fine band,
With clams on the drums, they're simply quite grand.
However, a seaweed gets tangled with glee,
Wobbling and wobbling, "Don't look at me!"

Crabs in their minivans, zooming through the surf,
Chasing the currents, they laugh with a smirk.
"Watch out for the octopus' crazy moves,"
They shout with delight, "he's got all the grooves!"

Under the silver glow, shenanigans run,
With sea creatures laughing, oh, isn't it fun?
Beneath the bright moon, where giggles do reign,
Every wave tells a story, a carnival's gain.

Melodies of the Azure Depths

In waters of turquoise, the mermaids convene,
Strumming on seashells, their charms reign supreme.
A fish with a bowtie sings tunes in the reef,
While rays in sunglasses just share in belief.

Haddock and haddock do a soft shoe,
While turtles in bowler hats cheer from their view.
They swirl and they twirl, with bubbles galore,
Creating a symphony right at the shore.

A whale with a top hat, he joins in the craze,
Swaying and sloshing in big, silly ways.
"Who knew the deep blue could be so alive?"
With laughter and dances, the joy will thrive.

With echoes of giggles, the ocean seems bright,
As melodies bubble beneath the starlight.
In the azure depths where the funny folks play,
Every splash is a chuckle, come laugh and stay!

A Canvas Painted in Seafoam Dreams

With brushes of coral and splashes of fun,
The sea paints a canvas that's never outdone.
A seahorse in shades of bright bubblegum pink,
Sips nectar from flowers, and pauses to think.

A clownfish in boots, oh, what a rare sight,
He curtsies to waves, "I can dance and take flight!"
The plankton applauding, they glimmer and glow,
While jellyfish spin like a whimsical show.

Each hue speaks a story of laughter and cheer,
As crabs juggle shells, well, that's very clear!
An octopus painter, with arms all a-swish,
Decorates each wave with a splashy pink dish.

In this seafoam world, as bright as it seems,
Every corner is pulsing with colorful dreams.
So come join the fun, where the ocean does scheme,
In the canvas of life, we're all part of the theme!

Voyage of the Sea's Wanderers

Sailing on a boat made of cheese,
With seagulls wearing hats in the breeze.
Fish swim by in a conga line,
Winking at us, they seem so fine.

A crab jokes about his lost left claw,
While dolphins dance, they're quite the draw.
We laugh and cheer, a silly crew,
Chasing waves like a big to-do.

Sunsets paint the sky quite strange,
As mermaids giggle, it feels deranged.
A turtle shares tales of far-off lands,
While jellybeans float with flowery bands.

We search for treasure, a chest of bread,
To feast and munch 'til we're well-fed.
Ahoy the laughter, the quirky cheer,
On this voyage, we conquer fear!

Beneath the Surface of Memory

Bubbles rise like thoughts, quite absurd,
Each one's a joke, you might've heard.
Fishy faces grin wide and bright,
Swapping tales from morning to night.

A starfish claims he's a dance champ,
With moves so bad, we all just stamp.
Crabs crack puns, they steal the show,
As octopuses juggle, oh what a glow!

Snorkeling tales of the heyday past,
We giggle and swim, what a blast!
The seaweed smells like mom's old stew,
We laugh 'til we can't breathe, oh what a view!

Memories dive, then pop like balloons,
Carried by tides and silly tunes.
With every splash, a grin shines through,
In this wacky world, all feels brand new!

A Mirage of Tropical Dreams

In a hut made of marshmallows and fluff,
We sip on drinks that taste quite rough.
Coconuts sing in high-pitched tones,
As we giggle at our silly phones.

The sand tickles toes, a pleasant tease,
While lizards play cards, with too much ease.
Palm trees flirt with the banana skies,
As colorful fish tie funny ties.

Sunbathing seagulls on floaty mats,
Roasting their jokes like summer chats.
A mermaid insists she can fly,
But belly flops, oh my, oh my!

Tropical dreams in a wobbly trance,
Feel like we're stuck in a dance.
With breezy laughter under the sun,
This mirage is pure goofy fun!

Resonance of Nostalgic Waves

The waves ring out like laughter's chime,
Echoing memories, so sublime.
Seashells gossip, they're quite the crowd,
Sharing secrets, and feeling proud.

A dolphin tells tales of old-time spree,
How he once danced with a big human tree.
They laugh about days of beach ball games,
While seagulls squawk with silly names.

Kites drift above in whimsical grace,
Caught in the tide of time's embrace.
We splash around like kids once more,
Finding joy embedded in ocean's core.

Every wave whispers a chuckle or cheer,
Spreading smiles, inviting us near.
With nostalgia tied to each ripple and sway,
This sea of laughter paints our day!

The Palette of a Distant Wave

A seagull stole my sandwich, oh what a flight,
It squawked like a pirate, a comical sight.
With mayo on his beak and crumbs on the breeze,
He danced on the shore, doing as he pleased.

The sun wore sunglasses, too cool for the day,
While crabs played poker, as if to say,
"We're kings of the sand, with shells as our crowns!"
Their laughter echoed around our beach towns.

A fish with a mustache swam by with a grin,
It winked at the waves, where all dreams begin.
With colors so bright, like a rainbow's delight,
The ocean's a canvas, creating pure light.

So here's to the waves, with their silly rapport,
They tickle our toes and then ask for more.
With jokes in the foam and laughter on the shore,
Let's dance with the tide, life can't be a bore!

Resonance of Nostalgic Waves

The waves ring out like laughter's chime,
Echoing memories, so sublime.
Seashells gossip, they're quite the crowd,
Sharing secrets, and feeling proud.

A dolphin tells tales of old-time spree,
How he once danced with a big human tree.
They laugh about days of beach ball games,
While seagulls squawk with silly names.

Kites drift above in whimsical grace,
Caught in the tide of time's embrace.
We splash around like kids once more,
Finding joy embedded in ocean's core.

Every wave whispers a chuckle or cheer,
Spreading smiles, inviting us near.
With nostalgia tied to each ripple and sway,
This sea of laughter paints our day!

The Palette of a Distant Wave

A seagull stole my sandwich, oh what a flight,
It squawked like a pirate, a comical sight.
With mayo on his beak and crumbs on the breeze,
He danced on the shore, doing as he pleased.

The sun wore sunglasses, too cool for the day,
While crabs played poker, as if to say,
"We're kings of the sand, with shells as our crowns!"
Their laughter echoed around our beach towns.

A fish with a mustache swam by with a grin,
It winked at the waves, where all dreams begin.
With colors so bright, like a rainbow's delight,
The ocean's a canvas, creating pure light.

So here's to the waves, with their silly rapport,
They tickle our toes and then ask for more.
With jokes in the foam and laughter on the shore,
Let's dance with the tide, life can't be a bore!

Lanterns of Light on the Water

The moon is a lantern, igniting the seas,
While fish wear tuxedos, just doing as please.
They leap with a giggle, a shimmering show,
We laugh with the stars, down below they glow.

The sailboat's a puppet, cuts through the night,
With wind as its partner, it takes to flight.
"Oh no!" shouts the captain, "I've lost my way!"
The gulls just chuckle and cheer in ballet.

Octopuses juggle with shells and with ease,
While dolphins perform in a splashy tease.
The waves tell us secrets in frothy delight,
As sea turtles groove to the moon's silver light.

Our laughter floats high with each wave's parade,
As lanterns of dreams illuminate the glade.
The night sings a tune wrapped in whimsical glee,
Where water and joy become wild and free!

An Ode to the Ocean's Grasp

The tide takes my flip-flops, a sneaky quick thief,
It giggles and dances, oh what a relief.
I chase after them, all wet and so spry,
The ocean just chuckles, "I'm just passing by."

Sandcastles stand tall, but here comes a tall wave,
It crashes with laughter, no fortress can save.
"Fear not!" says the sand, "I'm a fan of this fun,
We'll build it again, under the hot sun!"

The whale makes a splash, it's a rollercoaster,
It serenades fishes, a true party booster.
With waves full of bubbles that carry our cheer,
Ocean's a jester that draws us all near.

With shells as our trophies, we gather with glee,
The ocean's embrace is the best place to be.
So here's to the laughter, so buoyant and bright,
In the arms of this water, we find pure delight!

In the Heart of the Beach's Lullaby

The sand sings a lullaby, soft to the ear,
While hermit crabs dance with no worries or fear.
The palm trees sway gently, with rhythm and grace,
As coconut fellows join in the fun chase.

A crab playing maracas, with rhythm so neat,
The waves cheer him on, tapping out a beat.
"Let's party!" they chant, with bubbles and foam,
While jellyfish glow like they're calling us home.

The sun takes a bow, as the day starts to fade,
With shadows on sand, a magical parade.
Children all giggle, as they run from the tide,
For the beach is a playground, where joy takes a ride.

So cuddle the shoreline, embrace all its dreams,
As laughter and fun mingle with sunbeams.
In the heart of this backdrop, let joy reign supreme,
With the beach as our stage, we'll dance and we'll gleam!

Tides That Carry Us Away

The crabs are dancing, oh what a sight,
With their little claws waving, looking just right.
Seagulls are cackling, stealing our fries,
While we laugh and complain, watching them rise.

The waves keep crashing, our sandcastles fall,
As we giggle at seaweed, a green, gooey ball.
The tide pulls us in, like a playful child,
We hang on for dear life, both terrified and wild.

The sun starts to set, painting the sky,
We wave at the dolphins and let out a cry.
Their flips and their jumps, quite the weird show,
Making us question what we really know!

As night creeps in, the laughter won't cease,
With tales of the day's fun, we find our peace.
The tides may carry, but our joy stays here,
In this world of nonsense, we have nothing to fear.

Dreams Adrift on the Horizon

A coconut floats, or is it a boat?
We laugh as we wonder, will it stay afloat?
With visions of pirates, we set sail to sea,
But it's just a mirage, no treasure for me!

Our floaties are lopsided, we boldly declare,
Champions of wobbly, will we win this dare?
The sun's getting hotter, we're turning to toast,
Yet laughter fills the air, that's what matters most!

With dreams of adventure, we splash on the side,
Our snorkels are leaking, oh what a ride!
Fish pop their heads, and stare with surprise,
What kind of weirdos make waves with such cries?

As the sun sinks low, our giggles still play,
The dreams may drift off, but we'll smile anyway.
Tomorrow we'll float where the silly winds blow,
On dreams that are silly, but full of a glow!

Echoes of the Coastal Dusk

The beach chairs rock, set for a thrill,
As we munch on chips and drink our fill.
The crickets start singing their nightly tune,
While we try to dance under the watchful moon.

Our flip-flops flop, a chaotic parade,
With laughter erupting at every charade.
The stars are our witnesses, twinkling with glee,
As we argue which one looks like a 'Z'.

With shadows that twist, mischief's in play,
Ghosts of the sandcastles from earlier day.
We're chasing the waves as they sneak and retreat,
Only to trip each other right off of our feet!

As dusk wraps us up, the night's just begun,
With echoes of laughter, there's always more fun.
So here on this shoreline, we'll shout and we'll cheer,
With echoes of joy, we'll have nothing to fear!

Beneath the Palm's Caress

Under palm fronds swaying like dancers so bright,
We hide from the sun and ponder our plight.
A giant piñata with snacks is our aim,
But first we must figure out how to aim!

With fruit punch in hand, we concoct our own brew,
A splash of confusion is what we'll construe.
The ants have a party right under our toes,
While we laugh at their hustle and their tiny woes.

Here under the palms, the laughter won't cease,
As we try to nap, but wake up with a fleece.
The beach umbrella becomes our fortress,
We battle the sand, oh what a mess!

The sun waves goodbye, but we'll still remain,
With dreams of the beach and the joys of the rain.
In this cocoon of fun, we know we must play,
Beneath the palm's caress, we'll never sway!

Dreams Adrift on Salted Winds

Sailing with a rubber duck,
Waves whisper silly rhymes,
I swear it winked at me,
But maybe I'm just losing times.

Fish are plotting in the deep,
To steal my sandwich slice,
I chase them with my net,
Oh, what a tasty vice!

Seagulls laughing overhead,
Stealing fries from clumsy hands,
I throw them crumbs in jest,
Playing king of beachy lands.

Pineapple hats and sunblock smiles,
We dance like jellyfish,
With every tumble and trip,
Life's a zany, salty swish.

Shadows Dancing on the Waves

Beneath the moon's goofy grin,
Our shadows frolic and play,
Twisting, turning, zigzagging,
In a water ballet!

Crabs accompany our jigs,
They don their finest hats,
Underneath the starry stage,
Their dance moves create spats!

Waves are giggling, oh so loud,
Tickling toes in a burst,
We join the crustacean crowd,
In this charming, ocean first!

Kooky turtles cheer us on,
With flippers as their flair,
In this wavy carnival,
We leave our worries there!

Where the Sky Kisses the Sea

Clouds wear silly hats today,
While dolphins surf the foam,
They teach me how to flip,
And call that place my home.

Stars peek through fluffy quilts,
Dropping laughter like confetti,
The horizon waves hello,
And my heart feels ever ready!

Seagulls squawking jokes they know,
Like comedians on high,
They heckle passing sailboats,
As they drift on by!

The sun must be a jester bright,
With rays so warm and gold,
In this joyous sea of dreams,
No moment's ever old.

Embrace of the Endless Waters

In puddles splash the merry crew,
With hats too big, they flop,
We giggle like we've lost our minds,
In this never-ending bop!

Watermelons float with style,
They cheer us on from afar,
We ride banana boats, and clap,
Feeling like a movie star!

The tide pulls my sense of calm,
But also steals my drink,
I laugh, I shout, I splash around,
Who knew I'd grow to sink?

Big old turtles nod their heads,
To our rhythm, a loud cheer,
In this embrace of endless fun,
We toast to laughter here!

A Haven in the Wind's Song

Where seagulls squawk and sea-cows roam,
The sand's a couch, the waves our dome.
We dance with jellyfish, quite absurd,
While crabs join in, it's truly unheard!

With buckets full of laughter, we play,
Building castles that wash away.
The sunburned noses, a sight to see,
As we argue who's best, the wave or me!

A gusty breeze steals our hat with glee,
Chasing it down while sipping iced tea.
A picnic's a treasure where crumbs take flight,
As ants serenade us, "Perfect delight!"

The sunset paints a canvas bright,
With whispers of sea tales taking flight.
We'll leave the worries on the shore,
In this silly haven, we'll laugh even more!

Beneath the Drift of Currents

We drift like boats on a jelly-filled sea,
Where the fish throw parties, just wait and see.
The tide tickles toes and swirls with cheer,
While dolphins toast with coconut beer!

Beneath the waves, the crabs play poker,
While turtles belt out tunes that'll stoke yer.
Seashells whisper secrets too well,
In this watery realm, we're under a spell.

The sunlight flickers, we're never too shy,
As mermaids claim the treasure, oh my!
But their giggles betray stolen gold,
While our silly stories begin to unfold.

With every splash, we giggle up loud,
A symphony of chaos, a watery crowd.
So, let's dive deeper, we won't float away,
In currents of laughter, we'll forever stay!

Sailing Into the Unknown Horizon

We sailed a boat made of mismatched dreams,
With sails that flapped like an oversized beam.
Our map's upside down, we're lost, what a joke!
We argue if mermaids serve tuna or Coke!

With each wave's bounce, we giggle and squeal,
As sharks join in, giving a friendly heel.
The compass spins wildly, but who even cares?
Caught up in laughter, we're void of our fears.

A random island appears, it's made of cheese,
With a fountain of chocolate, oh, we must seize!
We feast with pirates, quite stylish and grand,
Turning sea-faring life into a dance band.

As we sail off into a sunset so bright,
Past the shadows of worries and into the light.
We'll write our own story of mischief and glee,
In laughter, we float like ships in the sea!

Chasing Ghosts of Fair Winds

In a twist of fate, we ride with the breeze,
Chasing odd ghosts that rustle the trees.
With goofy grins, we share a big cheer,
As shadows hold secrets of laughter near!

The ghouls throw a bash, with a skeleton band,
We dance with the spirits, hand in hand.
Their howls are like music, a whimsical tune,
Under the glow of a silvery moon.

A treasure map drawn in ketchup and fries,
Leads us to delights in disguise, oh my!
With each ghostly giggle, we join in the fun,
Living for laughter 'til day is done.

So let's toast to the winds, the quirks of the night,
Where the funniest phantoms bring joy and delight.
In the chase of the winds, through the laughter we weave,

Creating memories, oh how we believe!

Tales Carried by the Coastal Breeze

Seagulls squawk about the snacks,
A beach ball flies—oh, what a whack!
Children chase crabs, oh what a sight,
While grandma snoozes in sheer delight.

Flip-flops flip and flops them too,
Sandcastles rise, then start to rue.
A wave comes in with laughter's sound,
And beach gear flies all 'round the ground.

Ice cream drips down, a sticky race,
A seagull laughs at the quickened pace.
Each splash and giggle tunes the air,
With sandy toes, we're unaware.

As the sun dips low, the stories reign,
Of questing for the clownfish's chain.
Breezy whispers, oh my, what fun,
Each memory bubbles, like a tide run!

Threads of Horizon and Hope

A kite takes off in the sky so blue,
As Uncle Bob shouts, "Hold on—don't skew!"
The tail gets tangled upon a tree,
And everyone laughs, including me.

The horizon beckons with a cheeky grin,
While the ocean waves seem to shout, "Let's win!"
But still the sandwiches are run by ants,
As picnic finds new, conniving chants.

Laughter echoes through the salty air,
A jellyfish floats with a disco flair.
We strut and dance like the seagulls dive,
This coastal life makes us feel alive!

With each sunbeam, our troubles fade,
In mismatched hats, our plans are made.
Threads of joy woven tight and grand,
Stitching together this merry band.

The Lullaby of Forgotten Ports

Whispers travel on the salty breeze,
Tales of treasures lost to the seas.
A pirate's hat sits on a cat,
As if to say, "I'm where it's at!"

The old lighthouse blinks with glee,
As flip-flops dance near the knee.
Weathered boats rock with stories bold,
Of fishermen who might be sold!

A crab in a tux, a fish on a scooter,
Their nightly antics never fewer.
With each tale that floats through the night,
Laughter sings under the moonlight bright.

Forgotten ports, oh how you sing,
With mossy tales and a winter's fling.
In every evening's soft embrace,
We find our joy, our funny place.

Driftwood Stories in the Sand

Driftwood treasures wash ashore,
Each piece a story, never a bore.
Some claim it's a mermaid's lost shoe,
While others just laugh, "That can't be true!"

Sand dollars dance like money dreams,
While gulls make mischief with ocean schemes.
A turtle decided to join the fun,
With a surfer's hat—what a run!

Flip-flops thrown in a twisty race,
As shells declare, "Join our joyful space!"
Breeze whispers secrets, a giggling chant,
While the crabs plot mischief, oh how they plant!

Sandy toes and wisecracking waves,
Together they roll, like clever knaves.
This life, a canvas of laughter and cheer,
Each driftwood story draws us near.

www.ingramcontent.com/pod-product-compliance
Lightning Source LLC
Chambersburg PA
CBHW072118070526
44585CB00016B/1493